who Are You Calling Weird?

Marilyn Singer
Paul Daviz

words & pictures

Quarto is the authority on a wide range of topics.
Quarto educates, entertains and enriches the lives of
our readers—enthusiasts and lovers of hands-on living.
www.quartoknows.com

Text © Marilyn Singer 2018
Illustrations © Paul Daviz 2018

First Published in 2018 by words & pictures,
an imprint of The Quarto Group.
6 Orchard Road, Suite 100, Lake Forest, CA 92630.
T: +1 949 380 7510
F: +1 949 380 7575
www.quartoknows.com

A CIP record for this book is available from the Library
of Congress.

ISBN 978 0 7603 6339 3

9 8 7 6 5 4 3 2 1

Manufactured in Guangdong, China CC072018

To David Attenborough,
who's always been an
inspiration.
M.S.

For Keira, Katya, and Tom.
P.D.

Contents

A big-eyed lemur with magical fingers. A very smelly bird that climbs trees with its claws. A roly-poly, scaly creature that isn't a snake. A duck-billed, egg-laying critter that isn't a bird.

Are these animals in fairy tales? Are they invented by writers or mad scientists? Nope. These bizarre beasts are just as real as you are. Although they may seem strange to you, there's a reason for each one's peculiar features or behavior. So, come along, if you dare, on a trip into the weird and wonderful.

Explore rivers and oceans, grasslands and rainforests, swamps and deserts. Climb up to the tallest treetops and dig down into hidden burrows. Swim in the sparkling sunlight, and dive into the darkest depths of the oceans to meet these marvelous animals. You'll find out who they are and why they look and act the way they do. Get ready to be amazed at just how practical and fantastic the natural world can be!

Aye-aye

Nighttime. We are deep in a rainforest. Listen. Do you hear that tap-tapping? No, it isn't a woodpecker knocking on a tree with its beak. It's something much stranger. It's an aye-aye, rapping on a branch with its long, skeletal finger.

Because of its floppy, leathery ears and continuously-growing sharp teeth, people once thought the aye-aye was a rodent. But it's actually a lemur, a type of primate found only on Madagascar. Most lemurs are active during the day, but the aye-aye is nocturnal. Its huge eyes can see well even in low light and, unlike all other lemurs, it has that special middle finger which it taps on trees. It is listening for the echo that says there's a hollow tunnel beneath the bark. Inside the tunnel are tasty insect larvae. With sharp nails, the aye-aye tears open the bark and uses its finger to fish out its meal.

Aye-ayes can live in other environments besides forests. They often venture into farms and villages, where they feast on coconuts and other fruits. This makes them unpopular with farmers. Some people don't just dislike aye-ayes. They fear them. They believe that if an aye-aye points its finger at you, then you will die. So they think that aye-ayes should be killed before they can do harm. The truth is that humans are more of a threat to aye-ayes than vice versa. The only critters that should fear these gentle lemurs are bugs!

Pacific Barreleye

Down in the depths of the Pacific Ocean, it's hard to tell if it's day or night. Many fish that live there have eyes designed to take in as much light as possible. Some are so bizarre-looking that they're known as "spookfish." Among them, one species may be the spookiest of all. Not only does it have big, barrel-shaped eyes that can see in different directions—it also has a see-through head!

Most of the time, the Pacific barreleye stays motionless, its eyes turned upward watching for the silhouettes of prey above through its transparent head. But when it sees a target, the fish rotates its eyes forward and swims up to snag it. Its eyes are covered with bright green lenses that may help it spot jellyfish or other creatures that glow. The barreleye also uses scent to catch its food, sniffing it out through its nostril-type openings called nares.

A barreleye has a small mouth which lets it pick off prey with precision, including creatures caught in a jellyfish's tentacles. But these tentacles can deliver a wallop of a sting. The barreleye needs to keep its eyes on its prize, but protect them from harm. What does the trick? If you guessed it's that tough, fluid-filled, see-through shield that covers its head, you win. And so does the Pacific barreleye.

Dumbo Octopus

Some undersea creatures seem to have swum straight out of a horror or science fiction film. The dumbo octopus looks more like a cute cartoon character than a monster from the deep.

In fact, this charming critter was named for Dumbo, the elephant in the Disney film, who can fly by flapping his large ears. The dumbo octopus gets around by flapping its large, rounded fins. These fins allow it to move slowly on the ocean floor to find crustaceans, worms, and other prey. Like its relatives, it has eight arms, but the dumbo's are webbed. It uses them to steer, and it can also pulse them to move faster.

Sometimes, the octopus needs an even quicker means of escape. When a predator approaches, this mollusk takes in water and shoots it through its funnel, called a siphon, allowing the octopus to jet away safely.

There are seventeen species of dumbo octopus, and they are the deepest-dwelling octopuses of all. Small and sturdy, they are able to withstand extreme water pressure. Because of their appearance when they float, they are also known as "umbrella octopuses," but unlike your rain gear, an umbrella octopus stays permanently wet.

Star-nosed Mole

What if instead of seeing through your eyes, you saw through your nose? Then you might be a star-nosed mole.

Nearly blind, this extraordinary, energetic creature relies on the star-shaped organ surrounding its nostrils to find worms, insects, small fish, and other prey. Made up of twenty-two tentacles, the star is about five times more sensitive to touch than your hand. The tentacles are constantly wriggling, exploring, and sending messages to the mole's brain much as our eyes relay visual information to ours. In fact, the mole receives information so quickly that it can find and munch its prey in a quarter of a second. It is the fastest-eating mammal in the world!

The star-nosed mole is the only mole to live in North American wetlands. It uses its shovel-like feet to dig tunnels underground in order to find food. It also hunts underwater. There, the mole has another trick up its...nose. It can blow bubbles and then inhale them to sniff out prey, making it one of the few mammals able to smell things underwater. The star-nosed mole is a star in more ways than one!

Proboscis Monkey

A big, bulbous nose can be beautiful. Just ask a proboscis monkey. The male's colossal proboscis is designed to attract females. It looks impressive and it amplifies his mating calls, as well as his alarm cries that scare away enemies. The bigger the nose, the louder the calls. In the dense forests of Borneo—the only place where this creature is found—it's hard to be seen. It's easier to be heard, so loud is good!

Proboscis monkeys have partially webbed fingers and toes and are fine swimmers and divers. When they splash into the water, they can surprise both friendly visitors and killers such as the crocodile. The monkeys often must cross rivers to find the leaves and fruit that they like to eat. Their stomachs have special bacteria to help break down and digest their tough, leafy food.

Though they are now protected from hunting and capture, proboscis monkeys have lost much of their habitat and are endangered. Today, many of the remaining groups live in sanctuaries. There, they are safe to holler from the treetops and to enjoy a meal—as long as they push aside their big noses in order to eat it.

Hammer-headed Bat

If a big nose can make a call louder, imagine what a big head can do. Add to that a curly lower lip, a split chin, and a voice box that takes up more than half its body, and you too could make as much noise as *H. monstrosus*—the hammer-headed bat.

Twice a year in equatorial Africa, large groups of male hammer-headed bats gather together in the early evening to court their mates. They hang upside down in the treetops and bark. When the female bats arrive, the males flap their wings rapidly. If a female likes a particular male's song and dance, she'll choose him as a mate.

Because of their foxy faces, some bat species, including hammer-heads, are often called "flying foxes." But only the female hammer-heads appear foxy. They look nothing like the males and they don't make noise like them either. Like other flying foxes, hammer-headed bats are fruit eaters. They use sight and a keen sense of smell to find tasty figs, guavas, mangos, and bananas. Isn't that a mellow diet for a bat some folks think looks like a monster?

platypus

It has a bill and webbed feet like a duck. It lays eggs like a duck. It swims in the water like a duck. So it must be a duck, right? Guess again. It's a platypus!

A platypus is actually a mammal, and one of only two species to lay eggs. It has fur like an otter's and a tail like a beaver's. No wonder the scientists who first examined this creature years ago thought it was a fake—they believed someone had sewn a duck's bill onto another animal's body!

The platypus's front webbed feet and rudder-like tail help it navigate underwater as it searches for insects, worms, and shellfish on Australian river bottoms. Its bill has special cells for detecting the electric currents given off by its prey. The platypus also scoops up gravel to grind its meal because it has no teeth.

You might think it's safe to touch such a cute creature that can't bite, but beware! On their hind heels, adult male platypuses have spurs that can inject venom. Scientists think they may use them to fight off other males during mating season. Females don't have these spurs, but can you tell if you're getting close to a male or a female? Didn't think so.

Mwanza Flat-headed Agama

The red and blue Mwanza flat-headed agama looks like it came straight out of a comic book. As well as having flashy colors, it can walk on its hind legs and climb straight up vertical walls, earning it the nickname "Spider-Man lizard."

Only the males sport those brilliant colors. Dominant males are especially bright. They stay on top of the pack by fighting off other males. During these clashes, they bob their heads, chase, and bite each other.

However, these fellows don't always resemble Spider-Man and can blend into their surroundings when needed. They turn brown when they're startled, as well as at night. Like all reptiles, agamas are cold blooded and rely on sun and shade to regulate their body temperature. To keep warm at night they turn brown because this darker color retains heat better than the lighter, brighter hues.

The superhero Spider-Man has lots of talents, but only the Spider-Man lizard can change its appearance without having to put on a suit.

Hairy FrOg

There's more than one superhero in the animal kingdom—meet the hairy frog, A.K.A. Wolverine. When it is threatened, this small amphibian does something other frogs cannot. It breaks its own hind toes and sends out bony claws that can pierce skin. Don't believe it? Well, scientists handling this creature have the scars to prove it! No one is sure if the frog can retract these claws the way Wolverine can. Most likely its skin grows back to enclose its wounded toes.

What about the hairy frog's other unique feature—its "hair?" Although these African amphibians live mainly on land, they raise their young in water. After the mother frog lays her eggs, the father frog guards them. During breeding season, the male grows hair-like extensions on his sides which probably help him absorb extra oxygen so that he can stay underwater longer, protecting those eggs.

Many predators find both the young and adult frogs delicious. Those predators include human hunters in Cameroon and other countries, who capture the frogs with spears and skill. They have learned to avoid the razor-sharp claws of these astonishing amphibious Wolverines.

Boxer Crab

What do you do when you don't have teeth, jaws, or large claws, and everyone wants to eat you? A tiny crustacean called a boxer crab has the answer: fight off your enemy with a pair of living boxing gloves!

Found on coral reefs worldwide, anemones are colorful sea creatures with stinging, venomous tentacles. Tiny boxer crabs keep an anemone attached to each pincer at all times. When threatened, the crab jabs at its enemy with its living boxing gloves, or "pom-poms," as some observers prefer to call them.

Boxer crabs rely heavily on their anemones. They even use these helpers to mop up bits of food and dab the morsels into their mouths. Each crab keeps its anemones small by nibbling them. If a crab loses an anemone, it may steal one from another crab. Or it may create a clone.

To do that, the crab uses its legs to divide the remaining anemone into two parts. Then, presto, each part becomes a new anemone. What do the anemones get out of this? Perhaps food that the crab isn't eating, perhaps something else. Whatever the reason, it's an arrangement that works.

Pangolin

A superhero will tell you that a suit of armor is a good defense against a nasty villain. So would a pangolin—the only mammal covered in armor-like scales.

If a pangolin is threatened, it rolls up in a ball. Its scales are so tough that even lions and tigers can't bite through them. The pangolin can also release foul-smelling oil similar to a skunk's, which no predator likes. Unfortunately, it has a more dangerous threat than big cats—humans. Found in Asia and Africa, pangolins are the most hunted animals in the world. They are sought for food and for medicine. Some people believe their scales can cure several diseases and even protect against witchcraft and evil spirits. Pangolins are now protected by international law, but it is still difficult to stop illegal trade.

What do pangolins themselves hunt? Insects, mainly ants. They can devour around 70 million in a year! A pangolin has no teeth. It opens up ant hills with its long claws, then scoops up the bugs with its sticky tongue, which is longer than the pangolin's body—around 16 inches. When the pangolin isn't feeding, its tongue curls inside its chest. The pangolin may not be a superhero, but it does have super armor and a really super tongue!

Lowland Streaked Tenrec

You wouldn't think that an insect and the mammal that hunts it would have much else in common, but a grasshopper and a lowland streaked tenrec do. They communicate with other members of their species in a unique way: they rub body parts together. While the grasshopper scrapes its legs against its wings, the tenrec vibrates its quills, making a sound too high-pitched for humans to hear without special equipment. These spines are found all over its body, but especially on its head and neck. The tenrec is the only mammal known to make sounds this way.

There are many different types of tenrecs found in Madagascar, but the lowland streaked tenrec is the only species that lives in groups. Troops live together in a system of burrows and they vibrate their quills to stay in touch with other members of their group. Tenrecs may also be using these sounds to navigate through the dark forest undergrowth, much as bats use echolocation.

The lowland streaked tenrec has another use for its quills: self-defense. When it is threatened, it raises the spines around its head and neck. If the enemy doesn't back off, the tenrec will head butt the attacker. Nobody wants a face full of tenrec quills. Not even another tenrec.

Helmeted Hornbill

Did you know that head butting can be used for more than self-defense? In the forests of Malaysia and Indonesia, male helmeted hornbills crash their six-pound helmets together in mid-air to win a mate. The helmets are called casques. They are made of keratin, the same material as hooves, horns, and your fingernails. Female hornbills also have casques. They add weight to the beaks of both sexes, which helps them dig out insects from rotting trees.

Most hornbills' casques are hollow, but helmeted hornbills' are solid. That is the bird's advantage—and its misfortune. Helmeted hornbills are critically endangered. They are hunted for their helmets, which are carved into ornaments or sold as souvenirs. On top of that, their forests are being cut down to create farmland. Indonesia has recently announced a plan to save the helmeted hornbill, a creature which is remarkable in more ways than one.

Take the way it nests—when the female is ready to sit on her eggs, she enters a tree hollow, which the male seals up with mud. He leaves just a small opening through which he feeds her, while she nests in safety. When the eggs hatch, the female breaks out of the hollow, then she seals it back up until the chicks are ready to fly. Soon they too will use their casques for some hefty digging and maybe some serious head butting as well.

NarWhal

In the icy Arctic waters, real-life unicorns swim gracefully in large groups. These aren't the one-horned horses of myths and legends. They are narwhals, relatives of beluga whales, and their single horn isn't a horn at all—it's a sensitive tooth that can grow up to nine feet long and bend in any direction. Because it is covered with nerve endings, this tooth may detect and communicate information about the animal's environment.

For centuries, scientists have wondered what the tusks are for. They used to believe that males fought with them, but instead the narwhals just touch one another gently. Now, some observers think the animals use their tusks to tell each other how warm or salty the water is. The whales have also been seen using their tusks to stun cod. They hit the fish with their tusks then quickly gobble them up.

An Inuit legend tells of a cruel woman who was dragged out to sea by a narwhal. She turned into one, her hair knotting into a tusk. However, only fifteen percent of all female narwhals have tusks. Why? Don't they need to learn about their environment? Don't they like to eat cod? Scientists are still stumped, but they hope someday to discover the truth about the narwhal's amazing tooth.

Naked mole-rat

Picture a colony defended by soldiers and full of workers that tend to a queen's every need. All the queen has to do is produce babies—lots of them. You could be looking at a beehive. Instead, you're deep underground in East Africa, watching naked mole-rats.

This type of society is unusual for mammals, but naked mole-rats have other curious traits as well. Their eyesight is poor, so they view their world mostly through sound, smell, and touch. The soldiers chase off intruders, which they detect by scent, while the workers find plants for the colony to eat. They also create its complex burrows by digging tunnels with their oversized front teeth, which never stop growing.

These rodents are best known for their lack of hair. All mammals have hair, and naked mole-rats do, too but only about one hundred strands. Because they live in the dark and warm underground, they don't need fur to keep them warm or for protection from the sun. When it does get cold, they huddle together.

But perhaps most remarkable of all is their ability to live long and prosper. Most rodents have short lives, but naked mole-rats show little signs of aging and they can live for thirty years or more. Can scientists unlock their secrets to help people live longer, too? Only time will tell!

Hoatzin

You're near the Amazon basin. You want to see a hoatzin, so you follow your nose. Smell that? Now you know why it's called a "stink bird." The hoatzin's aroma resembles cow manure, and the bird tastes bad, too.

The smell and taste come from its diet—it's the only bird in the world to eat mostly leaves. The hoatzin has special bacteria in its gut to help break down the leafy food, releasing gases and giving the fowl its foul smell.

Perhaps even stranger than the hoatzin's scent and diet are its claws. Not the ones on its feet. The ones on its wings! The chicks' wings, that is. Hoatzins build their nests in trees overhanging rivers and lakes. When a predator such as a monkey or the weasel-like tayra approaches, the little ones use their claws to clamber out of reach. They can even drop into the water and swim until it's safe to climb back up. By adulthood, the birds have lost these claws—as well as the ability to swim. They can now fly, though not well. Despite this, they seem to be largely safe from predators, except for hawks and eagles. That may be because birds of prey cannot smell or taste hoatzins, while mammals most certainly can. One bite, and a monkey won't ask for seconds.

Kiwi

If you're a hawk that hunts by day, you use your sight to find your prey. If you're an owl that searches at night, your hearing comes in handy. And if you're a flightless, forest-dwelling kiwi, you need to use your sense of smell.

The nocturnal kiwi is the only bird to have nostrils at the tip of its long beak, instead of near its head. Kiwis use their nostrils to detect worms and insects that live underground. When a kiwi isn't hunting, it patrols its turf, marking it with smelly droppings and allowing only family members to enter. It will fight off rival kiwis by kicking them with its strong legs.

Kiwis typically mate for life. Their eggs are enormous—each weighing nearly one pound. She can lay up to six over a month which the male then incubates—sits on to keep warm. When the chicks hatch, they are covered in fine, hair-like feathers, and can feed on their own.

The kiwi is such a symbol of New Zealand that New Zealanders themselves are called "kiwis." But the birds are threatened by the loss of habitat and predators, such as dogs, cats, and weasels, that were brought to the country by settlers. A kiwi that survives these dangers can live for 30 years or more on a territory as large as one hundred and fifty football fields!

Leafy Sea Dragon

In the waters of Southern Australia, an extraordinary creature floats around kelp-covered rocks and beds of flowering seagrass, hiding in plain sight. You have to look very closely indeed to see the tiny, transparent fins and long snout and realize that it's not a plant, but an animal: a leafy sea dragon.

Believe it or not, the leafy sea dragon is a fish. It is a perfect example of camouflage—it looks like seaweed and blends in with its surroundings. Adult leafy sea dragons have few predators, but they've been threatened by people who collect them as pets. It is now illegal to capture these fish. However, they are still at risk because of pollution and habitat loss.

The leafy sea dragon is related to the seahorse. Like other seahorses, the mothers lay the eggs and the fathers care for them. But while male seahorses carry the eggs in a front pouch, male leafy sea dragons have a brood patch under their weedy tails. A female sea dragon can lay as many as 200 eggs. She transfers them into the father's patch, where he carries them for nine weeks. When they hatch, the young sea dragons face danger from predators until they grow their brilliant leafy disguise. Then, they too will float safely in the warm waters, looking like seaweed and hiding in plain sight.

Hairy Frogfish

When it's time to go fishing, you have to remember to bring your gear. But if you are a hairy frogfish, you never have to worry about forgetting your line and lure because they're attached to the top of your head.

Found in oceans worldwide, the hairy frogfish is a type of anglerfish, and like other anglerfish, it has an extra-long spine that resembles a dangling worm. The frogfish wiggles this bait in front of its face to attract other fish and crustaceans. Its mouth is so huge, it can eat fish its own size. Although the frogfish can walk on its fins, it doesn't move often. When it finds a good fishing spot, it will lie on the ocean floor for weeks at a time waiting until its prey gets good and close, then...gulp!

The hairy frogfish gets its name from its many hairlike fleshy spines which can fool enemies into thinking the fish is a stinging anemone. The fish can also change color to blend in with its surroundings and disguise itself as a sponge, a rock, or a clump of coral or seaweed. If this camouflage doesn't work on a predator, the hairy frogfish has one more trick—it can blow up like a balloon. Good luck to any creature trying to swallow that!

Three-toed Sloth

Some critters are always on the go and some are not. Of all these leisurely movers, none is slower than the three-toed sloth. It travels at around seven feet per minute—and that's when it chooses to move at all!

In South and Central American rainforests, three-toed sloths spend almost all of their time high in the trees, sleeping and eating leaves, shoots, and fruit. Sloths sleep nine or ten hours in the wild and much longer in captivity. Because they move so slowly, green algae has time to grow on their fur. This algae provides camouflage against predators, as well as food for the many insects that live in the sloth's fur. To spot predators, as well as mates, a sloth can turn its head almost completely around. But its only defense against attackers is its set of extra-long claws.

A sloth's claws have a powerful grip that allows the animal to hang upside down from a branch. When the sloth does climb down from its tree, these claws make walking extremely difficult. On the ground, it has to drag itself along on its belly, so it descends only to use the toilet or to take a swim. Sloths are surprisingly good swimmers. They move three times faster in the water and can hold their breath for up to forty minutes. What Olympian swimmer wouldn't envy that!

Human

Look, it's walking on two legs. It doesn't have any feathers or fur. And it's making the strangest sounds. What on earth is that weird animal? Why, it's us!

Human beings are unique in ways that other animals, if they thought about it, would certainly find strange. Take walking upright. It doesn't allow us to move as fast as many flying or four-footed beasts, plus it puts a strain on our backs. But it also frees our hands and arms to do many tasks. Then there's our lack of a warm coat. Without feathers or fur, we need to have clothes. But with so little hair, we also have fewer parasites than other animals. And while all creatures communicate in a variety of ways—some of which sound strange to us—people have speech. Talking can sometimes get us in trouble, but it can also get us out of it.

But what really sets us apart from other animals is our amazing brain. The human mind allows us to study and appreciate the world around us. It allows us not only to speak, but to create hundreds of languages. It is responsible for our sense of humor and our sense of fairness. Because of our incredible brains, we can find ways to protect and care for our planet and the many beings that live on it. We can conserve habitats, reduce pollution, and ban the hunting of endangered animals. We can choose to learn about these creatures and why they deserve to live here, too. Then we will understand that weird is just another word for wondrous.

Index

Further Reading

Visit the following websites to search for more information on these weird
and wonderful creatures and discover many more amazing animals:

National Geographic – www.nationalgeographic.com

World Wildlife Fund (WWF) – www.worldwildlife.org

New Scientist – www.newscientist.com

Science Daily – www.sciencedaily.com